COUNTERWEIGHTS

Counterweights

KESTRAL GAIAN

Reconnecting Rainbows

CONTENTS

Counterweights
3

Barriers
4

The Bridge
5

Thoughts on Take-Off
6

Horizon
7

Tunnel
8

Easy Jetting
9

Borrowed Paper
11

This Is Not Britain
12

Waendel
14

The Broken Bow
16

Into The River
17

Pied Pipers
19

Hello, World.
20

5th to Center
21

Six Seconds
25

Survival
26

Redundancy
27

Remnants
29

Looking Back
31

Change
33

Dawn Chorus
35

Shine
36

Chlorine
38

Crossroads
39

A Patriot's Act
40

Some Things
42

Left With Nothing
43

What Do They See?
44

Nothing is Untouched
45

Afraid of the Familiar
46

Simply Beautiful
47

Puppet
49

Echelons of Adulthood
50

In The Dark
51

Writing Poems Whilst Intoxicated Is Fun
52

Wake Up
53

Something Wonderful
54

Timing
55

Love and Hope
56

Sometimes
57

Why
58

Writer's Block
59

Routine
61

Comprehending Life
62

First World Problems
63

Eight of Diamonds
64

Disorder
65

Still
66

Mimic
68

Rusty Knife
69

What Next?
71

My life is...
73

Human Haiku
77

Birds and Humans
78

You Know Who You Are
80

The Topher Lesson
82

Revolution
85

This Page
86

I Don't Know Why
87

The Belle Epoch
89

The Old Lady at Breakfast
90

Walking Through Austria
91

I Hate 'Yes Men'
93

Sleeping Face
94

Comic Sans
96

Some People
98

Bad Light
99

The Irony of The Humans
101

We Met on The Train
103

Your Friend Always
104

Not Alone
105

ALSO BY RECONNECTING RAINBOWS PRESS - 107

Copyright © 2016 by Kestral Gaian

All rights reserved. No part of this publication may be reproduced, distributed, or transmitted in any form or by any means, including photocopying, recording, or other electronic or mechanical methods, without the prior written permission of the publisher, except in the case of brief quotations embodied in critical reviews and certain other noncommercial uses permitted by copyright law.

ISBN: 9781838342531

First Edition Published 2016
Second Edition Published 2022

This book's cover and chapter artwork were created for this publication by Malin Berg. You can find more of her art online at www.sleepimali.se.

www.KesGai.com
www.ReconnectingRainbows.co.uk

CONVEXITY

CONVEXITY

[k*uh*n-**vek**-si-tee]

noun.

1. Poems that are curved or rounded outward, looking out onto the world and all it contains.

COUNTERWEIGHTS

Perched insecure,
Atop a great height,
A triumph of man,
Over natural slight.

We perceive them as mighty,
These machines that we make,
Our superior knowledge,
Into plans that we bake.

Truth is we're fighting,
Trying hard just to mould,
The world that we live in,
To the dreams we are sold.

We build high, We build long,
And we architect wide,
We place all our hopes,
And our futures inside.

All of these structures.
Defiant to all,
Making us happy...
Until the day that they fall.

BARRIERS

Roads are tarmac,
Busses have wheels,
Cellphones have data,
Cities have crime,
Airports have fast food,
Politicians are traitors.

The more of the world,
that you dare to explore –

The peaks and the troughs,
the new and the lost,
the mighty and weary,
and fallen and cheery,

A familiar brand name
is always around...

Is this really how we want to
break the barriers down?

THE BRIDGE

Drawings are more than art.
More than
beauty.

Drawings are a window.
A sketch is a bridge.
A pencil mark an insight,
into the beauty,
complexity,
sadness,
and joy,
of an artist's mind.

THOUGHTS ON TAKE-OFF

(I)

It's amazing.
I've seen 36,000 feet on several
occasions of late -
and yet nowhere near
that many
shoes.

(II)

It's amazing.
I'm at 36,000 feet.
Again.
I won't make a shoe joke, though.
Nobody laughed the
last time!

HORIZON

Curve of the Earth,
or something to look
forward to?

Something old, or blue, or
borrowed, or new?

Breathtaking, stunning,
something beautiful to view.

Something to look upon together,
Something to travel with you.

TUNNEL

Tunnel.
Dark Tunnel.
Long Dark Tunnel.
Tunnel.
Cold Tunnel.
Endless Tunnel.

Tunnel
through which
a train blazes,
like a snake made
of fire.

EASY JETTING

One three six seats,
on this afternoon flight.
One three six stories,
in one three six lives.

One three six people,
dreaming one six three dreams –
All those perspectives,
all that love, all that greed.

One three six people,
some female, some male.
One three six colours,
some sun-tanned, some pale.

One three six faces,
some boring, some nice,
some people loving,
some hating their life.

One three six thinkers,
some dreaming awake.
One three six artists,
some write and some paint.

One three six eaters,
some hungry, some full,
some waiting 'till marriage,
some out on the pull.

One three six seaters,
fly high in the air,
carry one three six mosaics,
of love, life and hair.
Of flesh and of blood
and of nail and of bone –

One three six people,
just trying to get home.

BORROWED PAPER

Borrowed paper,
More like tissue,
I wonder what the hostess thought
it's use would be?
From a tree,
not like that I've bought.

Borrowed biro,
ink from favours,
I wonder what my friend must see
as I write?
In to the night,
the heart and thoughts of me.

THIS IS NOT BRITAIN

This is not Britain,
this big machine,
where logos light
the corporate dream.

Trains cannot
simply be,
they bear colours of
a company -

And what of buses?
No longer red.
Now they bear
adverts instead.

This is not Britain,
this I fear -
Community
has gone from here.

How else could we
have voted leave?
Pointing fingers,
Painting thieves.

Our melting pot
is boiling dry.
Tabloid headlines
full of lies.

This is not Britain,
and now I fear -
Sanity
has gone from here.

WAENDEL

What I see are swans,
sitting on the river,
As the sun slowly wakes.

Ducks swim around,
While the white swans stand,
Their feathers are caked -

Oil dirt and tar,
The animals live,
On mountains of litter.

I see water rippling
Impossibly glistening
Polystyrene like glitter.

There's a whole world below,
the water's slick skin:
It's a vibrant scene.

Fish swim about,
darting 'round rust.
And discarded machines.

They pulse and they quiver,
Past old concrete and steel,
Unaware of its purpose,

What once was important,
A minor distraction,
As they swim to the surface

Where sits a lone swan.
Surrounded by ducklings,
So black it burns.

Contrast so stark,
Chess pieces of creation,
drawing toward their final turns.

What I see is nature's triumph,
over man.

THE BROKEN BOW

Forgotten relics,
litter our land,
paths leading nowhere,
where greatness once planned.

A matter of money,
or political pride,
robs us of solutions,
foundations now hide –

reclaimed by the land,
that was torn before build,
prepared for a failure,
extracted, refilled,

Time passes slowly,
weeds start to grow,
The mistake – now a feature –
with few signs to show

that here there was something,
we all would have seen,
a landmark now lost,
to 'what could have been'.

INTO THE RIVER

Pages on the water,
fading away.
Like a tide of words.

Vowels and consonants,
bobbing downstream.
Like verbal pollution.

And so I sit,
an observer to it all.
My own creation.

I have contaminated
this river
with verse.

Given to it,
what it has given
to me.

As I watch,
the pages drift
out of sight,

and in among the hydrogen,
and oxygen,
are words.

My words.

Now lost

into

the river.

PIED PIPERS

The Peruvian flute band,
Is coming to stay.

Their music like quicksand,
Sucks time from your day.

It may not be tuneful,
It may not be cute,

But you cannot escape,
From the sound of the flute.

HELLO, WORLD.

I feel grounded,
feet firm.

And yet

The screen says I'm moving,
hurtling,
at 500 miles per hour.

Through the thick glass,
the world looks still.
Observed from motion,
obscuring thought, emotion...

This world is beautiful,
and yet,
cold.

5TH TO CENTER

Waste.
What a waste,
Resources spent.

Waste.
So much waste,
The metal is bent.

Plans.
Many plans,
For a city turned sour.

Plans.
All abandoned,
In the eleventh hour.

Waste.
What a waste,
This should have been good.

Waste,
What a waste,
If only we could.

CONCAVITY

CONCAVITY

[kon-**kav**-i-tee]

noun.

1. Poems that are curved inward, focussed on one's self.

SIX SECONDS

The tick of a clock,
The creak of a chair,
A constant reminder,
That someone is there.

Computers and clocks,
A truck that goes beep,
Proving to me,
That I'm not asleep.

Silence so black,
Yet deepest of blue,
Lonely yet shared,
Old, and yet new.

A world that keeps turning,
A world filled with ink,
Lost in a moment,
Makes me stop and think -

Silence is rare,
We don't give it time,
Perhaps we're afraid,
Of what we might find.

SURVIVAL

The key to the soul
is light
not like the butterfly turned sour,
turned evil.

Flutter away into the corporate
canopy of man-eating plants,
of dream eating trees.

Don't look back on it with sadness -

You invested in the bank,
and this is merely evolution...

Survival of the sickest -

Our ever failing economy.

REDUNDANCY

Perceptions, preconceptions -
we all judge one and another,
a constant stream of
mind-making
before the book has even opened.

Word of mouth
with word of man,
a combination only serving
to destroy,
even when it creates.

And then we watch,
watch and wait -

With judging eyes we
selfishly
count our eggs,
dismissing the dismissals,
daring not to care.

What else to do?

Human nature - number one
always before number two.

REMNANTS

You say sunshine, I say rain.
You say sky, and I say there's no way
to catch the ship after it's sailed.

Political bewilderment and freedom of speech,
too bad that a democracy is just out of reach.
There's no way,
to get back in after you've bailed.

You know that you're living
in the shadow
of the remnants
of a lie,
When you look up at the storm clouds
and below them is the sky.

Idiotic lawsuits and legal fees -
"We're here to serve you sir, we,
just want to please",
there's no way,
you're ever helping me.

Like puppets on a string we
live out our lives,
we act out fairy tales,
we don't even ask why.
The mold can never be broken,
it can only be bent.

You know that you're living
in the shadow
of the remnants
of a lie,
When you look up at the storm clouds
and below them is the sky.

LOOKING BACK

Is it wrong to miss
what we no longer have?
Looking back to days gone by-

When you're past the abyss,
and through all of the pain,
There was love that I could not deny.

I will feel it forever,
in this way and that,
as I think of him now and again,

I felt free as a feather -
but it wasn't forever,
and for months now I've had to abstain.

Moved on and smiling
we both seem to be,
and yet something will always be there

However, it's trying -
when the thought comes to me,
about how much we both used to care.

I hope they were true,
when they said that time heals
as I'm ready to give it a try,

I'm happy for you -
yet this is still how it feels,
looking back to days gone by.

CHANGE

There are days
where you feel,
really feel,
how deep your heart is -

You can feel it's walls,
look from the top down
and get vertigo.

There were times,
times I felt
really felt,
that my empty heart had broken -

I could feel the rupture,
Full of it's own broken shards,
Irretrievable.

But right now
my heart feels,
really feels,
like a stormy ocean -

Full, yet choppy
on perpetually changing tides,
spun about by you.

DAWN CHORUS

Neon cuts the dawn,
Just as voices from the past
cut the darkness,
and pierce the soul
with a blinding light.

Cold becomes warm,
White heat and blue waves,
Sparing not the weak,
Nor the mighty,
But the love of the common man.

As one world wakes from slumber,
Another feasts,
And another shuts down 'till morn,
Yet, here is dawn...

Cut by neon, man and his
Creatures of creation,
His not-quite-nature,
His empire,
His sick rose.

SHINE

People will stare
as you step into the limelight,
A shining example
of beauty and brain.

People will cheer
with you and for you,
At every corner
and round every turn.

People will smile
as they see all the things,
that you can do
and you can achieve.

People will wish
through jealous eyes,
that they could be there
doing what you do.

Now is the start,
it's all ahead
but all so easy

to grasp.

People don't know
just how bright
you can really
shine.

CHLORINE

We cleanse water.
Clean the ineffable cleaner,
Remove this
and that.

This 'cleaner' water.
It leaves me smelling worse,
far, far worse
than before I entered.

A chemical bath.

CROSSROADS

I lie here the most happy
that I have ever been,

To my left there is beauty,
to my right is a dream.

The dream makes me yearn
and has done for an age,

To my left there is beauty,
to my right a new page.

A PATRIOT'S ACT

Who watches the watchers?
Who watches the damned?
Who stands up to gaze
over their best laid plans?

If the tall and the mighty
who have fallen with pride
looked down on our nation,
what would they decide?

Institutions once mighty
we look on with shame,
The poor and the wealthy
are all throwing blame.

There are so many days
when things just feel gloomy,
Ministers evil,
scandals a-blooming,

Tabloids are frenzied,
hysteria looms,
telling us all
that we're certainly doomed.

They say now's the time
to feel courage and pride.
Patriotism
we usually hide,

But how can I stand up -
and proudly proclaim;
"This history of empire,
it brings me no shame!"

The truth is much harder
a thing we must swallow,
A history lesson

today and tomorrow -

Patriotism
does nothing for me,
nor the poor or the needy,
the caged or the free.

So let's tear down the walls,
and proudly proclaim;
"I'm done now with borders,
we're one in the same!"

SOME THINGS

There are things in this world
we dread...
Selfless and selfish,
static and in flux.

Some things can be fixed -
Death, disease...
Fear of what we know will come,
but that we can never change.

Some things we wish for,
like love, hope...
Fear that we will lose
the things we desire most.

LEFT WITH NOTHING

Scorn is a powerful word,
when you've done wrong
or tried to do right and failed.

Sometimes love is scorned.

Love is a powerful word,
like scorn but good.

When love is scorned, the good
and the bad cancel one another,
and you are left
with nothing.

WHAT DO THEY SEE?

I'm scared of the flowers. They look at me with disdain.
What do they see in the meadow, green?
Rumbling fiends - like the dying breath of man.

We pay, in the end.

We all pay, a sacrifice:
Bloodshed,
world wars,
slavery, poverty...

Battles for survival.

Yet the only real victim,
of our freedom so slain,
is sat in the garden,
staring at me
with disdain.

NOTHING IS UNTOUCHED

There is no such thing
as untouched nature.

Every flower's been smelled,
every tree climbed,
every bird spotted.

And yet, we lie.
And try,
Try to convince ourselves
that we're the 'first' ones here.

The only ones to see,
to know beauty.

We lie because we must.
Because of our need.
We lie to ourselves
to protect our very essence.

Our human nature.

AFRAID OF THE FAMILIAR

I want to go outside,
but I'm afraid.

Of the dark?
Sort of.

I'm afraid of the
familiar,
the places we know well.

New frontiers promise sanctuary.

Old frontiers harbor stagnant memories,
fragments of a past life,
waiting in the darkest shadows.

SIMPLY BEAUTIFUL

Love is confusing.
Not love for G-d,
which is always simply beautiful,
but love for people.

Old love, that re-ignites when
you see someone again,
for the first time,
in years.

New love, all mixed up
with emotion.
Silent love - love you can
never admit.

Sometimes I think,
if man just loved G-d alone,
life would be much simpler.

But then, that would deny
our very human nature -
G-d meant for us to fall in love,
I believe. And love can never,
never ever,
be wrong or bad.

PUPPET

If someone made a puppet of me,
And had it live out my life,
for a day, on a tiny stage,
I wonder...
Would people enjoy watching it?

ECHELONS OF ADULTHOOD

Why put off until tomorrow,
what you could do this very day?
It's not lethargic, but at times
life seems like a nagging parent.

If we are but a child to time,
running errantly through it's mercies,
feeling the years but never the seconds,
Then a time must come where we all rise,
And stand equal with time,
The echelons of adulthood.

Just as a child will swear
never to become like those who raised it,
is it too inevitable, that we must
all ascend to the heights of hypocricy?

Do we smash the glass of the pocket watch,
Or forever frolic
in a land of deadlines?

IN THE DARK

Tired ramblings
that I can't even see,
On a page so dark,
could mean anything.

I write not so it
can be seen,
more so that it can be
felt.

WRITING POEMS WHILST INTOXICATED IS FUN

Why do poems,
have to rhyme?
I try to write them
all the time.
I find it hard,
and quite restricting,
so I'm writing a poem,
to put odd words in.

Orange! Ha! Rhyme with that!
Purple! Wait, there is one, but it's not exact.
Anyway, my point is this:

WAKE UP

Sometimes you hear a sound,
intruding into your dreams,
a sound so real, you wonder...
Who's there?
What do they want?

But then you realise,
The sound came from the other side
of the wall. An echo from
another's life, another world.
Telling you it's morning there too.

SOMETHING WONDERFUL

It's funny.
You live life ignoring
the big empty hole.

The one you feel
every day.

It takes something
huge and strong,
and big and mighty,
and knowing and good,
and lovely,
to see that the hole was never empty -

you just had to find
the wonderful thing
inside it.

TIMING

People say the eye is
the window to the soul...

And yet, when you catch
someone's eye,
someone new,
you both have your guard up.

Never letting on.
Waiting,
watching.

Timing.

Turning to a stare.

Turn away.
Look back.

Repeat.

LOVE AND HOPE

Why do we love,
the things that cause us pain?

We 'put up'
and 'live with' -

we 'manage'
and 'cope.

Why don't we
'love' and
'hope'?

SOMETIMES

Sometimes words come,
like a river's ebb and flow.

Sometimes there are
no thoughts I can show.

Sometimes I'm too busy,
to write, think, feel sleep.

Sometimes I'm too rushed
to get very deep.

Sometimes I get worried –
Am I an adult, or child?

Sometimes I feel ashamed –
Am I a moron? Too mild?

Sometimes I'm a showoff –
Trying too hard to make friends,

Sometimes I'm a loner –
and shy away to the end.

WHY

I write
not because I must.

I do not write
for acceptance,
or skill,
or praise.

I write
because it is natural.

I pick up a pen
and I write –

Not because I must.

Because I can.

WRITER'S BLOCK

Today it seems,
I have found,
that when I try,
to be profound,

to write a verse,
from the heart,

I'm shocked –
I seem to have
some writers block.

It turns out life,
often unfair,
has shaken me,
got in my hair,
and now I cry,
but cannot write,
I don't know why,
I have this plight.

I want to pen
a lovely rhyme,
to get across
these thoughts of mine,

I cannot -
I seem to have
some writers block.

ROUTINE

Isn't it funny how we lose so much?

All our creativity.
Our imagination.
Our passion.

They ebb slowly
through the cracks –

The cracks we create
for ourselves...

As we fall

ever mindlessly

into

routine.

COMPREHENDING LIFE

Human life is hard
to comprehend –
We are each, individually,
closed off beings.

Tiny.

Cages of flesh,
clinging to a rock,
alone in the vastness of existence.

And yet...

We are all connected.
Without each person's
uniqueness,

Each person's contribution to the world,

Empires may never have been built,
Wars would never have been fought,
People would never have been loved.

FIRST WORLD PROBLEMS

We seem obsessed
with the transfer of energy.

We eat and sleep
to work and earn
to get paid
to live in a house
with water and electricity,
so that we can
eat and sleep
and charge our phones

and tweet

about how hard life is.

Priority? Wrong.

EIGHT OF DIAMONDS

Diamonds can be
strong and mighty,
Diamonds can be beau,
Diamonds can reveal
a beauty,
Diamonds sparkle so.

Diamonds eight can
make a wedding,
Diamonds eight bring class,
But diamonds eight will
live forever with
spades and clubs
and hearts.

DISORDER

There are times that the mind
needs to hide away.
Never telling the reason,
never quite back to stay.

In absence it spins you
great stories to say –
a boy who's connected,
a young man's new day.

So you live out these stories,
that your mind leaves for you,
until it returns,
and starts life anew.

STILL

On becoming still
you become aware.

Movement.
Movement everywhere.

Every pattern,
all around.

Movement.
Voices, lights and sound.

The rising sun
lights up this book.

Golden.
Golden unmistook.

The colours warm,
yet my eyes burn –

Golden.
Golden, then I learn:

You cannot sit
and simply watch.

Progress.
Progress marches on.

MIMIC

Industrial graffiti.
A cacophony of shapes,
smells,
sounds.

So rhythmic, purposeful,
they take on a life of their own.

Mirroring us – our creations.
In our own image,
laid bare.

RUSTY KNIFE

Sitting here wasting away,
I think of previous things.
Got to clean out the garbage,
left by shattered dreams.

I sit and count the hours,
I sit and count the years,
From one moment to another,
I need a change of gear.

And I think it's about time,
I got off the starting line,
I'm ready to start living my life,
Instead of picking at my dreams with a rusty knife.

Don't want to be stranded,
Stuck in a rut these days,
No more 'what if' or 'if only',
Time to give some praise.

Time to stand up and be counted,
Stand up for what I believe,
Stand up for freedom, stand up for justice,
Stand up and I will be free.

And now I know it's time,
To leave that starting line,
If life's a race then I won't finish last –
Now, to forget the past.

WHAT NEXT?

One looks forward,
and yet,
is the sum of all
that is behind.

Empires once mighty,
they fell – and yet,
in doing so
gave birth

to the new.

Had Newton loathed trees,
Mozart never played,
Hitler never hated...

Would any of us
be here

to live, to love, to learn?

We are the sum
of a world of choices.

The only question
that matters is –

What will we choose to do next?

MY LIFE IS...

Uncatagorically,
Unequivocally,
Irrefutably,
Unrecognisably,
Inconsolably,
Unabashfully,
Undeniably,

Simple.

COMPLEXITY

COMPLEXITY

[kuhm-**plek**-si-tee]

noun.

1. Poems that are interrelated, emotion-charged ideas, feelings, memories, and impulses.

HUMAN HAIKU

Creature of habit.
Normality consumes you,
'til the sun last sets.

BIRDS AND HUMANS

Birds soar,
Soar around the crimson moon -
Flutter, pulse,
Gone too soon.

Birds sing,
Sing out their hearts desire -
Chir-rup-ing,
In midnight fire.

For birds and humans,
Were meant to be together
Whether on land or sea.

Their wings take flight,
To us it seems,
Birds embody our every dream.

Birds perch,
Perch high above the ground -
Observing life,
Both lost and found.

Birds know,
Know that their lives are short -
Moving, flying,
Creatures of thought.

For birds and humans,
Will always be together,
Whether on land or sea.

Their wings take flight,
To us it seems,
Birds embody our every dream.

YOU KNOW WHO YOU ARE

When the sun rises in the west,
The best of all your troubles
come to shine –
not that you'd ever find the time.

Morals so loose you can
hear them rattle when you walk –
your lies have always been the talk

of the town. Every news beat,
on every new street,
and weathered shore:
they never bore.

My eyes are sore.

One life is never enough
To live all of the lies you've told.

One life will never be enough,
to bring back all the dreams you sold.

Why should I bother?
Tell me.
Why should I care?

In spirit, you are always there.

Watching. Waiting.
I despair.

One life. No more time to share.

THE TOPHER LESSON

I don't know the time,
It's late but that's fine,
Lit only by the kitchen light,
Fan casting shadows in my sight,

It's quiet yet I hear a roar,
As I see him sleeping on the floor,
My ears are pounding and I'm sure,
He's one my heart is crying for.

It's like ice surrounds my veins,
Cutting through capillaries of fire,
It's like a knife right through my brain,
My heart rate just keeps getting higher.

It's getting really hard to think,
I want to swim but all I can do is sink,
In to this,
Part pain, part bliss.

Part of me feels wrong -
And not because it's unrequited,
Part of me is turned on -
Even though I'm trying to fight it.

I can't control this,
I wish I could.
I can't control this,
I think I should.
I wish I could.

And it's like ice surrounds my heart,
Cutting through the fire of feeling,
No ending, no start.
My brain is numb, my body reeling.

It's getting really hard to think,
I want to swim but all I can do is sink,
In to this,
Part pain, part bliss.

Wait.

Why should I complain?
I'm lucky to have a heart to feel with!

Wait.

Why feel disdain?
Love is a thing that surely must be celebrated?

Unrequited love may not be easy,
But it makes the world go round -
For a world without love would surely crumble
into pieces on the ground?

And it's like ice, and fire and rain,
Returning to feeling alone again,
Feeling my happiness run and hide -
It's hard when love is person-blind.

But that's part of life -
I guess.
I'll get myself out of this mess.

That's life -
After all.
What's left to do but rise after the fall?

REVOLUTION

What did you expect?

The trees are the same,
The sky is the same,
The birds sing the same,
The world is the same.

The only difference between
today and yesterday is the girl,
stood outside,
Looking up at the window.

The last trace of a revolution
in her eyes.

THIS PAGE

This page left blank
Intentionally.
For reasons why?
Not all can see.

Perhaps a statement
This empty page,
Advice that's missing,
No proverbs sage.

Perhaps it's wise,
From time to time,
To refrain from writing,
A single line -

The boldest statement,
That man can make,
A page left empty,
Not by mistake.

I DON'T KNOW WHY

Please don't answer,
don't reply,
I love you
but I don't know why.

It seems so
clear to me now,
I love you
but I don't know how.

Don't be angry,
don't get mad,
I love you
but it makes me sad -

To think this thing
I feel, for shame,
my love for you
will cause you pain.

So do not listen,
close your ears,
for my love for you
will last for years.

THE BELLE EPOCH

No matter how cultured,
Or enlightened we be,
We all make assumptions,
Based on what we see.

We judge based on colour,
It's sad but it's true,
We assume different culture,
Or religion to you.

We judge based on gender,
Perceive women less strong,
And forget it's a spectrum,
No expression is wrong.

We judge based on movement,
Claim dancers are gay,
Yet mechanics? The contrary.
All straight, we would say.

We call ourselves cultured,
In an enlightened age.
No. We're just children,
Unsure how to behave.

THE OLD LADY AT BREAKFAST

A smile is infectious.
It changes ones image,
abates and corrects
the impressions we form.

A smile is a signal,
Shows our true colours,
calming and peaceful
on a cold frosty morn.

WALKING THROUGH AUSTRIA

There is a drunk.
There is a drunk man.
There is a drunk man on the floor.
There is a drunk man on the floor outside.

In the rain.

Wearing nothing but yellow underpants.
Talking nothing intelligble,
in a language I barely know.

I sit with the drunk.
The drunk man.
The drunk man on the floor.

I talk in pieces,
in a language I barely know.

He smiles.

I felt like I understood the words.
I felt like I understood him being on the floor outside.
I understood the rain –
and felt like I understood the city.

The one thing
from my time in Austria
that I still do not understand –

What possesses a man
to go out drinking,
wearing nothing
but
yellow underpants?

I HATE 'YES MEN'

Click of a pen,
pushing out ink.

Resolute, yet expectant,
telling you what to think.

Click – yes, I'll sign that.
Click – yes, by nine.

Click – yes, I can.
Click – yes, that's fine.

Indeed the pen is mightier
than the sword,
for it has the power,
to enslave is all,

If we are not careful,
And do all that we can,
We'll each all be trapped,
Living as a 'Yes Man'.

SLEEPING FACE

A sleeping face
can look peaceful,
can look angry,
can pout.

A sleeping face,
can change,
can look happy,
can look out.

A sleeping face is a mask,
behind which you find,
A billion dreams,
Locked away in the mind.

A sleeping face
is an ever changing
mask of truth -

Discarded on waking,
Forgotten, uncouth.

Thoughts and feelings,
We ought to embrace,
We can learn so much from,
A sleeping face.

COMIC SANS

I laugh at funerals,
You're the one in black clothes,
I'm there making light,
But everyone knows:

While I'm smiles and sunshine,
You'll be down below,
With your sad, sombre melancholy,
Lights turned way down low.

Through this cacophony of
ever-changing ups and downs,
I wonder if I'll make you smile,
Instead of always making you frown.

Opposites we -
You and me -
Living here in such disharmony,
Never feeling calm, you see -

Criticism banned,
You shut out things that you can't plan.

You're Times New Roman,
But I'm more Comic Sans.

I'm always positive,
You're always play-it-safe,
I'm always "doesn't matter",
You're always assigning blame,

Don't see the point in helping others,
What are we to do?
I find it difficult,
When you can only think of you.

Opposites we -
You and me -
Cooped up hating one another,
Like some perverted soap opera.

Should we change the channel?
Or stick to our misguided plans?

You're always Times New Roman,
But I'm more Comic Sans.

SOME PEOPLE

Some children grow up with hope,
And dreams.
But not every child,
Not this child,
Not me.

Some people have things to reach for,
They need to aim high.
But not every person,
Not this one,
Not I.

Some households have love,
And people who care.
But not every home,
Not my home,
Not there.

Some lives are so happy,
And filled up with smiles.
But not every life,
Not my life,
Not by miles.

BAD LIGHT

We say "it's bad light" when we don't love,
The vibrancy of the colours of the world above.
We photoshop everything, We fake, and we fudge.

But things look okay,
By the light of day.

We cover our skin in oils and in paints,
Convinced we must make ourselves look more like saints.
We butcher, Inject, Remodel and Taint.

But things look alright,
In natural light.

We have this most unnatural notion,
All of these plans that we must set in motion,
Size zero, image, obsession, devotion.

But how great things seem,
With a natural gleam.

I weep when I think that this is how we raise,
A whole generation to behave.
We're unique creatures, not fashion slaves.

And we all look okay,
By the light of day.

THE IRONY OF THE HUMANS

Humans make this world ugly,
Humans make this world blue,
Our idea of society,
A socio-normative flu.

It gnaws at the fabric,
And uniqueness of life,
The beauty of nature,
The native wildlife.

Humans come to life empty,
Our minds quickly filled,
With stereotype and prejudice,
And who must be killed.

Humans murder each other,
and say all the while,
we know there's a reason,
for violence and bile.

Our meaning is muddled,
Our truth has digressed,
We distort it with lies,
That add lead to our chest.

And yet we can dream,
Of love and of peace,
We long for a world,
Free of war and disease,

A new way of living,
For all, not just some,
If only we knew,
How to put down the gun.

We need them for peace,
We need them for war,
The reasons for either,
Not known any more.

So we follow a pattern,
As humans we do,
We hate and hate over,
Finding reasons anew,

To kill one another,
And destroy our own Earth,
And poison our children -
As we dream of rebirth.

WE MET ON THE TRAIN

The way you act,
The subtle ways,

The things you say,
How you behave,

They tell me much,
Of who you are,

A DC Gymnast,
A Superstar.

You play it well,
The confident role,

The ray-bans and clothes,
Concealer on that mole,

But when people aren't looking,
Your gaze does betray,

The lonely abandon,
You feel every day.

YOUR FRIEND ALWAYS

Times may look bad,
And so fill of woe,
Like you're in a bottomless pit.

On days like that,
It's so hard to know,
That life isn't complete shit.

But this I want to speak anew,
I present to you a different view.
Life is pretty wonderful when you're able to be you.

Oh, how you are amazing,
A truly valued friend,
All my thoughts of happiness,
 to you I'll always send.

It won't always be easy,
Some days may feel quite sad,
But always try to be yourself,
And I promise you'll be glad!

NOT ALONE

Rolling hills, stilted clouds,
Like the child who laughs aloud,
Until his father stops him, proud -
Dumping rain onto the ground.

Human creations pass us by,
Things of beauty, but a different kind,
Fellow travellers tut and sigh,
As I sit here and wonder why.

Blocks and shapes of iron and steam,
Breaking the hills as the wheels below scream,
Proof that someone had a dream,
A changing world in which we gleam.

Yet here I sit on a fabric throne,
A train full of people, all traveling home,
Not knowing a soul, but together we're thrown -
Through the hours and the miles, I am not alone.

ALSO BY RECONNECTING RAINBOWS PRESS

Poetry
TransVerse: We Won't Be Erased
(Anthology) (ISBN: 9781787234093)

TransVerse II: No Time For Silence
(Anthology) (ISBN: 9781838342517)

The Boy Behind The Wall:
Poems of Imprisonment and Freedom
by **Dalton Harrison** *(ISBN: 9781838342524)*

Emotional Literacy: Collected Poems and Song Lyrics
by **Ash Brockwell** *(ISBN: 9781838342579)*

Young-Adult Fiction
Hidden Lives
by **Kestral Gaian** *(Second Edition) (ISBN: 9781838342586)*

CPSIA information can be obtained
at www.ICGtesting.com
Printed in the USA
BVHW091722090922
646655BV00008B/433

9 781838 342531